SEP 0 4 2009

All Odd and Splendid

wesleyan poetry

HILDA RAZ

All Odd and Splendid

Wesleyan University Press
Middletown, Connecticut

Published by Wesleyan University Press, Middletown, CT 06459

www.wesleyan.edu/wespress

Printed in the United States of America

5 4 3 2 1

Library of Congress Cataloging-in-Publication Data

Raz, Hilda.

  All odd and splendid / Hilda Raz.

    p.   cm.   (Wesleyan poetry)

  ISBN 978-0-8195-6892-2 (cloth : alk. paper)

  I. Title.

 PS3568.A97A44 2008

 811'.54—dc22   2008027418

NATIONAL
ENDOWMENT
FOR THE ARTS

A great nation
deserves great art.

This project is supported in part by an award from the National
Endowment for the Arts

Wesleyan University Press is a member of the Green Press Initiative. The
paper used in this book meets their minimum requirement for recycled
paper.

Everyone today looked remarkable . . . so absolute and immutable down to the last button feather tassel or stripe. All odd and splendid as freaks and nobody able to see himself, all of us victims of the especial shape we come in. —DIANE ARBUS

CONTENTS

IV. Seeing the Changes

V. The Especial Shape

VI. All Odd and Splendid

1

HISTORY

Everyone today looked remarkable

Vocation

Light comes in the window, must be seven A.M.,
time for breakfast, but the aroma traveling up the staircase
is roast turkey and now that you've opened your eyes on the window
light is dim, so it must be coming through the open door.
Crouched in the window, chiaroscuro, leaning back on the screen
a bent guy in a hat, his face lined with dark,
bends forward into the room and smiles. No, he's laughing
and then he whispers, "I've come for you, it's time."

And you decide—now that you're awake you know
you can do it—to negotiate, maybe not now,
you're only eight, but later when you're twelve,
no, thirty, so far off, and he nods,
he's amiable enough, affable
as you'd hoped he would be.
And then he is gone.

You get up—didn't you used to have pink sheets on your double bed—
same price as the twin and more flexible for the future, who said that?—
but they seem to be blue percale, royal blue with red and black stripes,
and while you're brushing your teeth in someone else's bathroom,
maybe the one in the Belgian pension where you celebrate your birthday,
you decide to go swim in the dark waves, no, maybe the dining room
where you'll order puffy pancakes with apples, or strudel, or maybe

you should write a book someday,
shouldn't you write a book, shouldn't everyone
who has met death in the window and put him off
for a while write a book?

Diaspora

The gates were closing and the time was late
in spite of our efforts in the car,
our suitcases packed, our coats tossed off,
goodbyes said, or not to be said

in spite of our efforts in the car
the houses closed, the plants farmed out
goodbyes said, or not to be said
the neighbors told, the little ones in their beds

the houses closed, the plants farmed out
the station doors opening on uniform corridors
the neighbors told, the little ones in their beds
we fanned our faces, opened our books

the station doors opening on uniform corridors
then there was smoke, and damp, and sky
we fanned our faces, opened our books
we shut the windows, began to move

then there was smoke, and damp, and sky
our suitcases packed, our coats tossed off
we shut the windows, began to move
The gates were closing and the time was late

Childhood

She wove my hair in braids
before each day began.
I tore each plait apart
on the walk to school.

My clothes were always clean,
dresses each worn twice:
pinafores starched stiff
by hands not quite my own.

Daisy diagonals, white and gold,
marched up and down on blue.
Left to right, up and down,
the windows between in curtains.

The weight that bore us down
was air that could be fire.
Our uncles walked the roofs
binoculars to their eyes.

At night the shades were drawn.
Cannel coal filled the grates.
The winter cold meant ice
and blades to skim the pond.

Heal marks on linoleum
meant rubber for the war.
We crushed the cans quite hard
their labels first soaked off.

We filled white cardboard boxes
the size of small dolls' coffins
with brushes, paste, and cloths.
The red crosses on the lids
Meant something we don't know.

Water Ceremonies

1.

To pour. First, to lift the heavy pail.
Let us consider morning,
a child cross-legged on a tile floor
bent over the water garden. She
wears a flowered apron over shorts.
She half-fills emptiness to leave room
for the half measure of light
to fill up every iota of space,
replaces the lid carefully
to balance on the lip of the vessel.
Who is the beneficiary here?
We ask her but she doesn't say.

2.

To lead and delegate. First, to name
the Club with code, initials only.
Then to find a mission:
all girls against all boys.
We vow to like all girls
no matter if they are mean or good,
to hate all boys
no matter if they are kind or bad.
You, Carlotta, are fearful and must not be.
If you will change, sign here.
If not, resign. Here is a line.
You, Veronica, will be first.
You will make decisions.
If you so choose, sign here.
If not, resign. Here is another line.
We ask you only for your pledge.
Here they drink.

3.

To lift up. She takes one side,
I take the other. The heavy waves.
Together we catch the ocean.
If we are careful, we can carry back
what's salty to the berm of the wall
we've made, pour out the water
to make a moat. She takes one side,
I take the other. So our childhoods pass.

4.

To go on. Then I knew he was odd.
His arms too long. His hip thrust at a twist.
He balanced on the fountain, walked the brim.
Splashing to the center he could stand on one leg,
but his eye was cast. He was born with a caul.
What could I do? Already he was loved.
His voice in the morning fluted
a name. He knew who I was.
Others might cast him as ugly.
I gave him a halo, bent to praise.

All Odd and Splendid

The especial shape we come in
is insufficient, says the child
come slippery from the body
of another especial shape that comes in
the shape of its mother. Giving birth
is no treat, let me tell you, she says.
The nobody born will become somebody made
but the surgeon on duty just then
was entering tenth grade as the crisp nurse
sponged out the child's eyes. Splendid,
thinks the special shape called the mother
reaching out her arms. The child, unchanged,
begins to cry. Excellent, says the nurse
handing over the child. Nothing odd about it.

Wilt

When the phone rings
Aaron says *hello*
and I ask, what are you doing?
He says, *building orchid petals*
out of thin sheet silver.

Now I know something important
about the body
left behind in shards
which seem to have melted
into the body of my child.

Then my mother
from her temple of brain
says something to her daughter
about rain and rocks something
about the shape of earth
as night pulls a skullcap
over the mountains.
She seems to want me to notice sky
as a wave of salt and pepper hair
falling over an eye, something that winks.

Son

He is always saying and telling me
something urgent in the same tones
I use when I am telling him something
urgent but nobody is listening.
We are alike and unalike.
I like him I do.
He says he likes me
So what's the problem.

The problem is birth.
What an opera,
the lights, the dais,
the cast of characters wearing
the same gown.
We're both there
forever. I am.
Where is he?
He's left the building

Entered the stadium
where the team is getting ready
to tear each other and everyone apart.
Is he garbing up? He says no.
But I can see his pads in the backfield
still skin on the cow's back. Io,
I think and he laughs.

He Graduates from Clown School

"A lot of what I thought was magic
is habit," says Aaron,
chewing his nails. He wears
one red Chuck Taylor on his left foot
a black on his right. He reaches up
to adjust his wooden horns,
shrugs sequins straight on the vest
under his tux jacket then pulls on gloves.
Presto, his hands are red puffy leather.
Trots fast down the grassy knoll, drops
into a green pit where his teacher
bows, straightens, smiles, and calls out,
"Give me your best shot and hug me after."
The crowd around the rim cheers.

Aaron is ducking and weaving.
His dark face shines. He is walloping, punching,
crouches and POW! he uncoils, connects,
all his energy building and disbursing
until he seems to explode

twenty Good Will china cups
on the floor of the garage.
I watch rage doing its work.
What girl wouldn't give
a good night's sleep
for the chance to break china
with her mother's blessing?

But that girl is this boy now
who wears boxing gloves
in a natural ring with his teacher
who is hitting him back, POW!

and nothing I can do—was there ever?—
will stop the fight
or these men from making
the hits land hard, head to head,
to prove something to themselves,
to the watching crowd, to us,
about men and their exclusions.

He/She: The Bike

Aaron is leaving
or is he coming home?

One woman I am, or the girl,
hitches up her socks, clips
one corduroy pant leg close
and unlocks her bike. Soon
she'll be flying down the hill
we hiked up.

It's time to split
myself into two women,
or no, a woman and a girl.

Aaron has left the door open
behind his new backpack
hitched up on his shoulder
as he bends to enter the car.

I am pushing up the hill
what someone promised was wings
as he turned a wrench in the spokes
and bolted together new life.

Credo

I believe in the vision eight months
into your change
us side by side
you in your green pajamas
your brother's head bent
past my shoulder to the book.
I hold your small hot body
against my breast
as I mother of sons
Cornelia and her jewels
read on. My right arm is around you
the newest entry in our family
Bible. Your new name will be written. I will write it.

We read. Your small brother
is building a tent over us
where he lies
still as an accident
his bones knitting
until he is mended
a grown man. And you still not here yet.

In my vision I slept
you within me my knuckles
raw from worrying the tent flaps closed
next to your brother who was lifting them.
You were growing. I knew that my body
could hold you as long as necessary.

Spring Snowstorm

Each hour of day fills, excessive and pure,
with snowfall through the eyes of windows;
all color spills down walls of each room.
The bird bath has a cap of twenty inches.
And still snow is coming and the light
greyer under the pines and spruces
out the east window. The swings
are quiet under a pile of ash white.

Under this snow, gathering itself
in ditches, in hollows of needle fists
where robins already have begun
to build, the earth must be inflamed.
Yet I can't see it, only the stasis
of the ground beneath the movement
of snow falling. This day is the first day of spring.

Snow falls through the hours
of the day long after the hours of the night
and we have been told snow will fall still
for another slice of time, up to the pickets
of the far yard and beyond.
This first day of spring
someone is five years old.
Someone else is seven.
And the one whose words
I have been reading all afternoon
the one whose flesh is falling from his bones
somewhere in Ohio, his voice is speaking.
The flakes are tiny now in the gathering cold.
The veils wind flings over the junipers
merge into a milky silk.

All day I have been sitting and reading
the words of students who themselves
are playing at soldiers in the drifts, ordering
their lives with snowmen and pizza, beer
and whatever touching they do. For a few hours
alive in this excessive and pure place
snow comes and comes, replacing the sight
of earth in spring with layers of wet. If I refuse
to breathe, I can hear the germination of wild carrot
in the ditches outside of town. If I refuse to breathe
all beauty will be cold and remade forever.

Dante's Words

What did he call her that day? A woman
who was only his mother, bound by time
as a semblance of a woman
who could be more, a woman
unbound, more manly than light
nature allowed women?
She didn't weep. She was a woman
born of Holocaust, cold
to what's transitory, cold
insults hurled by women
as he still was then, her lovely stone
child, a woman hard as stone.

Now he is a man, stone
muscles, the soft breasts of a woman
gone entirely, his refashioned chest, stone
musculature fashioned by hours stoned
on lifts, endorphins, an ever increasing time
at bodywork, focused, intent, his eyes the color of stone.
She is the mother. Her heart, a long-buried stone
under her breastbone, beats out the pace lightly
only for herself. He has become his own light,
his steps never faltering. The light
he sheds is a beacon, a luminous fire-stone,
son, a specific against season's cold,
oh warming child, a human son, running in the cold.

Or so I think in these long months of winter in my cold
garden asleep under its mulch. Wrapped by stone
fences, the bird bath is upended on the patio cold
against ten clay pots emptied of earth, cold
snow filling their mouths. The empty fountain, one woman
in stride, is emptied of her geraniums, her cold

belly filling with snow, the residue of dirt underneath a cold
scrim against her clay apron. When will time turn
to refill her body—this year with herbs, thyme
and rosemary— to make an apron of cold
leaves against the heat? Her fountain waters, all light
at play, overflowing a cascade, will be sunlight.

Nearly morning. Spring chill through the window. Light
begins to enter the room where I sit, cold
in my bathrobe, waiting for the light
to warm the room, to seep through the linen nightdress,
light to cover the body old as the library stones
just starting to gild on their plinths, the lions in sunlight
rosy at the horizon. In these hours, oh Light,
come as I sit writing, alone, a woman
fretting, fretting as a woman
does, about her son, his flight home, his living room light
clicked on this dark morning miles away as he packs to come
      home in time
for more life, more darkness, more sunrise, more time.

What is time
bound this morning with light
hinges? Time
that seeps through our bodies, time
that scatters, dissolves, washes cold
rivulets down the leather bindings, time
of restoration, spring, time
to gather the straps, the phylacteries, to number stones
on the graves, the grave markers, the heaps of stones,
each one brought by a mourner, in remembrance of times
spent heart to heart, the breathing ribs, the whispers of women
at work together, the making and undoing, the binding,
      the woman.

The grey woman
who planted her garden in stone,
this woman, her flesh cold
in this early morning cold,
still weaves her silks and linens. She stays still, early morning sunlight
crosshatching the loom, the pages, the garden, our sons, through time.

Sunday Morning, without Couplet

I am wanting to die. Therefore I turn to
books. Someone will tell a story, start to finish
fear, hatred, weakness, then gain to begin
toward the end, conclusions and wisdom. I am
so hungry to live in the world of sunshine,
star patterns, veils of birth, nebulae from space!
Breathe, breathe, breathe, breathe, walk out
to the fence between neighbors: one died horribly.
The new people yell, scream obscenities I hear
above the voices of their children, who thrive.

Tyr

My children, the stories always say, *One god with one hand, one god
    with one eye.*

In this story, Odin is the god with one eye,
his eye traded for a drink from the well of wisdom,
the well of wisdom guarded by a frost giant.
"What will you take in exchange for a drink?" asked Odin.
"I'll take your eye," said the giant. And he did.

So Odin became the one-eyed, all-seeing, all-knowing god.
Everyone knows about Odin.
Tyr is his brother, the one you don't know yet.
The silent one. Our hero.

In the beginning, Tyr was the most important god,
the guardian of oaths. You'd swear by Tyr,
the god of keeping promises.
But the most famous thing Tyr did,
he told a lie. The lie he told saved the world.

Once a giant wolf called Fenrir was going to eat the world.
None of the gods could stop him. This wolf
was stronger than all the gods put together.
So the gods asked Odin, "What to do?"

Odin said, "Fly to the spirits of the earth, the gnomes
and the worms, the dwarves and the Norns,
and the gods of fate and ask them for this exactly:
a bond that can't be broken."

The spirits of the earth in reply made an oxymoron.
They took everything in the world that was impossible:
the breath of a bird

the beard of a woman
the sound of a cat's footstep.
And more you will remember for yourselves.
And they wove these things together
to make a fetter softer than silk and finer than thread.
And all the gods lined up and tried to break it.
Of course they couldn't, not even Thor, who was their strongest.
And the gods of the earth said, "This is a bond that cannot be broken.'

Then, my children, the gods invited Fenrir
to Asgard, their home, for a gala party.
And they said to the guests, "Let's play a game."

Fenrir was the son of Loki, the god of tricks,
who hadn't been invited, of course,
since he wouldn't want his son to die.
And death was the outcome, don't you think?
A party game was the best they could do without Loki,
the only subtle one among the gods,
a kind of trickster, we would say, an entertainer.

To Fenrir the gods said, "Here is a bond that can't be broken.
We're strong. Let's all try to break it!"

Fenrir suspected a trick but he was very vain,
very strong and he wanted to eat the world.
So he picked up the bond and pulled on it
but nothing; it doesn't break.

The Norse gods may not have been very subtle
but they knew how to flatter. They said,
"With your fine body and strong muscles
you can break it, you're so much stronger than we are.
We'll wrap you up in the bond and you flex one time,
like the Hulk, it'll fall right off. We believe in you."

Now Fenrir isn't as smart as his dad,
but he knows a trick is somewhere at the heart of this story.
And he knows the gods really hate him.
And, my children, he hates them, too.
Besides, he doesn't want to eat the world before Thursday.
He says to the gods, "If I can't break this bond, will you let me go?"

And the gods looked at each other and they said, Yes,
having learned something from Loki.
"Promise?" says Fenrir, the wolf.
What do you think they said?

Now, my children, here is the crux of the story.
A lie is the foundation of civilization.
If you can't trust someone to keep their promise,
what can you trust? The ties that keep up the heavens?

Fenrir asks for proof. And the gods thunder,
"Are we not the gods? Is not our promise our bond?"

The wolf says, "Maybe. But one of you step up.
Put your sword hand right here, in my jaws.
You'll let me go if I can't break the bond!"

The air around grew quiet.
Once the wolf is bound, he is bound.

Tyr, the quiet one, stepped up.
He lay his hand down in the wolf's jaws.
Fenrir can feel Tyr's strength. He feels his fingers,
his entire sword hand in between his teeth.

Then Fenrir lets the bond that can't be broken
serve as a noose to tie him up.
And Fenrir feels his own strength.

But of course he can't break the noose
because it's not made of anything at all.

The gods walk slowly away down hill, have lunch, and play dice.

And that, my child, is why we have a planet to call home,
and why Loki, father of Fenrir, came to hate the gods,
and Tyr became the god of strength
since he learned what he had to do to save the world
and then he did it.

And Tyr is also the god of truth
who has only one hand, his left hand,
which he has learned to use well, as some of us do.

And the heavens? The vault of the sky still hangs
steady above us although we pierce it often
with our arrows and our mortars; clouds drift
at evening between us and the stars. Try to hear their stories.

II
THE TRANSFER OF POWER
So absolute and immutable

Once

he made the decision, he packed up
the car, wrote notes of instruction
about the furnace, the extra filters,
the air conditioner, the location
of the humidifier. REMEMBER TO BRUSH
THE KIDS' TEETH, he wrote in soft lead pencil,
all caps, and turned to pull open the door.
Only then he remembered his razor. The others slept on.
This house was my house, he thought, the tiny sounds
of damp breathing, the early finch against the screen,
flame peonies he'd planted by the breezeway
letting go their ants. So he took a minute more to take up
the menthol lather, to his chin, then under, and then
the blade.
                        When she woke,
he was gone. She stretched, pointed her toes, rose
and slipped through the door. His side of the cabinet
was empty, everything gone as expected,
but in the creamy bowl, under curds of lather,
a rusty shine, his blood waiting for the sponge.

Storm

The harsh winds blew the snow into a froth,
the snow into a pile, a noose around the house
that bound the front door tightly closed.

The couple stayed indoors and slept a night,
a longish day they waited while the sight
of each ground out a fury. What to do?

They hated what they saw. The heated room,
the glowing stove, the bread dough rising
on the glassed-in shelf. He'd had his fill
of flesh, of winter's cheer at mid-day, gloom
at early dark. He wondered where they were,
familiar home, familiar two, their cat
he'd loved for roaming, home to lap
at milk that's warmer than bright ice. Now dark:
the wind, the troubled pair at table, silence
in and out of doors. They knew the month
was rounding somewhere else to mud and birdsong.

And then it broke, the weather warmed, a rush
of melting filled the pond, the window wells, the backyard
fountain, found the untiled chinks, moved bricks
that lined the paths, uncovered bulbs, made fingers ache,
and backs, then freed the driveway then the earth.

They rose up early, worked like men with men
to find that place renewed, in each. Then went.

The Transfer of Power

Let's say, they'd say
for years beginning a game.
Let's say the general's aide
decamped with the wife
of the general. Let's say,
the stage director ran off
with her manager. Let's say,
they said and began a genre.

So let's say you're getting to the point
where day has fewer hours, no, let's say
fewer sunny hours to play in the garden
with the soldiers, most of whom have lost
their heads. Let's say you've got to settle
down on the trip to Kansas behind the swings,
settle for the night at least, here's the fire pit
where we left it last winter let's stay here.
The soldiers' heads belong to the maidens
or the shoals of fish offshore, we saw them
swimming the Hellespont on Friday, after gym.

Pack up the boxes, boys, dinner's over.

Let's say I'm getting to the point where you've got
to take over. You've got to pick up the slack,
pay the bills, shovel the driveway. The doctor waits.
The borders are insecure. The flour in the tin, weevils.
Firewood is scarce and the mule's eaten. Open up
and get ready, let's say, for the next chapter, the curtain.

An Evening

In the church,
a concert hall for the evening,
a son sits shoulder to shoulder
with a microphone he's rigged
for this occasion, premiere of songs,
his music set to her words, two poems,
ten years between the writing.

                         A small metal square
set between prongs on a music stand, this recorder,
an emblem of their time together
so many years apart, so many days.
Sound waves break on the metal membrane.
Of course she cries. The audience applauds.
Her heart seems to open its fist.
Which words are set to his first bellow?
The voice of the mezzo soars over the beat
as wind outside whispers to the city streets
and rain freshens the pavement for its cabs.

Infant, in New York

Not quite brand new, four weeks
from birth you begin to grin, to coo
for your father who sings back your vowels
exactly in German nonsense as he swings you
easily in an ellipse around his sturdy body.
You flop. Or almost, but you're caught

in time. You frown. Fourteen days from now
at six weeks you'll laugh out loud. Your mother
in her milky daze catches your eye as you whiz by.
Her German diminutive, a word for shark, refers to
your meeting her body, which next you do. Our oh,
your liquid sounds at breast, stock-still, relaxed,
define you newly arrived after a three weeks' delay.

Your long starfish fingers wave outside a blanket
of purple microfiber that catches shine from light
to throw it back, on us. It's you who breaks our silence.
We're listening. We speak to you the first of many sentences.

Visit

Booboo is what they call her, baby round-face,
blue eyes squinting under straight red brows her daddy's
baby Booboo
nobody but a stranger.
Spiky red hair a halo.
All gums when she smiles.
She bounces and waves. She grunts to let you know
grunt back. Teaches you language.
Waits for your response. Grunts. Grins.
Fusses but doesn't often wail.
Is she smart as her parents? Who knows. Probably.
Seven months.
What was her daddy at seven months? Twice her size.

Which says nothing of her sister, Booboo's sister, clambering
onto the high seat of the swing on the hill. Letting loose.
Or traveling to the tree park to pick the bird's cherries.
Then afraid, climbing the splintery wooden slide
to the top, touches then holds tight the cold metal bar, over and over.
Climbs onto a lap for a story, someone in the lead she's following.
Other stories she sings to herself lying down on the coral tile in the
        livingroom,
everyone else in the kitchen. Or curled on the cold slate of the hall still
        singing.
We make a spoon necklace same as the kitten's in her book.
Mama is patient and cares for them all.
She herself is a big sister who says when we ask,
that at school she is Anna Link, almost reading.

Four/Two

She's pulling my toes,
scraping my skin, opening
my blood, eating my fingers,
she says of her sister.
Great giggling. They're both
talking at once on the telephone
six hours away by direct flight.
They've been sick and we're recovering.
Ohh, says one into the phone, she's
trying to open my butt, she always
does that. Screams of laughter.

Eva Unwraps a Bandaid

She's three and bleeding
From her thumb. She shows me
Where Lego Horse snagged Truck.
She asks, can we go to the cabinet?

I hold her up to reach the mirrored door,
Lift out the box from the shelf.
With one hand she opens the lid, retrieves

What's needed. I put her down.
She tears the side of the paper by the strip,
Opens the wrapper, pulls the tape.
I shape the gauze around the cut
And kiss her hair.
                        She never smiled.
Not once. Nor wept. Nor does she now.

III

WAR

Button, feather, tassel or stripe

Complaint

What about air fast   then static
or thick in the lungs of the infirm?
And concrete stairs designed by folks
without degrees, what about engineers?
Milk was sour in the hot coffee,
first specks then curdle and the last in the jug.
Brains spew facts then shrink or were supposed to
be gathering specifics for eons. What about heart?
Can be fixed oh yes or replaced
but pain   worry   recovery
down slow halls. What about it?

The perimeter of the new patio
all sand and also sand between bricks.
Jump and it disappears. Nothing but holes.
And then fall. Everything emptied   no standing pools
birdbaths turned over   pot saucers upside down
fountain turned off and dry. But rain's in the reservoir!
What about mosquitoes during a hot spell? What about breeding viruses?
The long kind and the short. What about them?
The pet has no food. And says so, again and again.

And what are YOU doing about it? What?
Watching birds? Magpies? A rusty colored wren
with flush at the breast? What kind of dove
you've never seen before? A hummingbird
with a rosy bib? All tiny body invisible wings
sucking up red sugar water from the feeders.
Oh. I get it. Diversion. Something heard from a burning bush. A hum.

Flight

The flight was fast through darkening clouds
building cell on cell. The air was cool
in the cabin. The movie, a musical,

quieted our alarms
with costumes, all fringe and jewels.
The flight was fast through darkening clouds

growing, towering, then blowsy
trailing wisps, settling flat on billows.
In the cabin the movie musical

went on; we sat rapt. At least I did,
twisting my rings. No longer the fool.
The flight was fast through darkening clouds.

And then the air outside was glowering
and the steward said by microphone *fast cooling*.
In the cabin the movie musical

stopped, then resumed. *Tighten your belts*. I did.
In the vents something howled.
The flight went fast through darkening clouds.
In the cabin, the movie musical.

The Public Baths

What passes for soap is marble here
where light is candles at night or by day
the piercings in walls. Steam. Flutes. Harps. Boys
singing or humming. The deep gutturals
of conversations. Tenor overtones.
Pubic curls and linen towels. The one
who limps leans on the one who whispers,
Apples, guava, smoke, salt. Parchment wilts
in the wet as the ink runs sand. Where
is a scribe when you need him? Sir,
take my hand. What happened? *The war
was annals of transportation over mountains,
you could say we tried everything new
for the leader, or that a mother's curse
rebounded and he was born with a caul,
you could say that women are evil
or that the hem of one born of one can never
be whole.* Look to your right. Such disaster
of flesh. And the brain a beacon. You
all here, sodden and bold in the heat, consider
this: if one shall be broken, the other increase.
Eat flesh and rejoice. The bounty of the fields is next.

Pets

The yard man is exactly the age of his dog,
six years, which is thirty-seven, he says
between lips chapped and swollen
from what he's been doing in the truck
with his helper. The dog waits,
the yard waits, filled with its pales
and spikes.
        The dog follows so closely
at his heels. Why? He must be afraid
of being left behind, which must have happened
a time or two in the years he's been cherished.

What is a pet? Some thing
breathing, that's one. Some thing
warm, that's another. Something
to curl over when the world shuts
down for the night, or is it the body
shuts up, so tired, so ready
to exchange air freezing for
the warmth of . . . whatever is
in the bed, that pet we're discussing
as we fall down the lines here?

Pet, have you been cared for
long enough? Maybe not,
cold weeks alone in the nest,
a bucket by the bed, that whimper
from you as the others romp
and roll belly up for the scratch.

Whoever we are, surely we deserve
the moment each day when our eyes clear
to see that the loved face is ugly,

the hips turned inward, the fur patchy,
the eyes protuberant and blind,
the gait unsteady, don't we?

And that other one, who turns his back
on the scene? He always shows up again,
so we know he loves with keen hunger
and would adopt, take home, and set out for us
a bowl filled with every kind of kibble made
from tallow and the leftover flesh of our kind.

September 11

My sneakers, having taken me through a bed of poison ivy
to the window, now transfer their oils to the bathroom rug
and no wonder in this time of monstrous trouble
I have knocked five times on the glass, and you have come

to open the door, for which anyone would be grateful,
your bristly head bent to the knob, round glasses reflecting
light from the glass of water that tips as you brush by,
intent on my call, so the spill sprays over the teak

in much the same way as the physics of matter
determined today that marble and steel would vaporize
or turn rubble under such pressure. Meanwhile, I'm inside
the door, returned to our hearth where the fire

place holds ivy, the summer having just closed down
and the grate in the basement covered with dust
isn't ready to be hosed down, isn't ready to open her arms
to keep us far enough, but not too far from the blaze
that we ourselves have set, unwisely,
in a house made of twigs and straw.

Fire Should Be Measured by What Didn't Burn

National Public Radio News

Passion is inferred by what isn't said.
Absence will be valued by the one who notices first.
Pleasure can be ranked by all other thoughts kept out.
Fatigue is always spoken in a narrow range of voice.
Wars are justified by the troops who didn't die.
Progress is best measured when sleep shuts out the rain.
Fidelity is most natural when the ear believes in pressure.
Hunger is most keen when the menu spreads like ice.
Will takes up its post when the mind is bent on territory.
Resolve will turn to weeping when the curtain falls at last.
Lapis cracks but slowly as pearls are ground to dust.
Medicine's no specific unless the alternative is rust.
Sacrifice can have no meaning if the witness turns away.
The field is only battle when the mess hall shuts its doors.
Wind brings down the enterprise, no matter our delight.
The crowd moves toward the exit when the puppet master speaks.
We put our shoes on standing if our beds are board and brick.
We search the web for meaning if our dinner table's bleak.
A life's measured value is who didn't come to call.
Noise can best be noted by the silence afterward.
Death can have no meaning. That's what we learned in school.
Your going into silence is the thing we can't endure.
Whatever comes will come. Leaves are flying in the cold.
The flocks about their maps. The cord wood in the frame.
We've made the best we can of the absence and the void.
The furniture of living's exquisite. Believe it. Say no more.
Keep all the curtains open. In the window flies the snow.

Paper Strip

I mustn't spill over
margins. The desk
isn't mine to foul I'm
writing in ink. In fact
country mine white
slick one side rigid
boundaries nothing
organically loose to
grow in the body or
dirt. Formal rigor
for pen and brain.
Why have I come
to arbitrary limits?
Everything lovely
is discipline: borders
time, dedication. Okay,
why did the phone ring
& ring & ring in the emp
ty house? Where are you?
Fallen air from the slippy
surface of the reverse? Oh
page be my friend. I need you
to guide my thoughts on loss
exactly the opposite of absence
which I think may be death
this page filled up completely edge to

IV
SEEING THE CHANGES

Arousal

CN, d.12/04

Season of lights   the usual round.
Where guns emit light darkness is.

We can lay the cloth for supper.
We can intuit the blessing.
We can light candles, multitudes,
ever again the sappy stars.

The heat comes on like flannel.
Our aches dissolve   a sucked water.
Out the window birds in some distress
flying or hitting the window.

Only earth retains her usual shape,
her cones leaking, her rounded places
flattening, her crust where the bulldozer digs
giving way for the coffin, this one.

We trust the body to soften   to flare
to moisten   to be changed under pressure.
Where you are writing we are waiting
for the ink to dry   for the stalk you are to rise.

Coma

By dying she comes closer to peace
or peach, the color of her skin,
a message from the future
when her eyes the color of the respirator
open on a mad world where she'll dwell a while.

We watch her settle slowly back into sense,
hear her unaided breath hitch and catch,
smell her slide into an animal self
test the air for scat
as she drags her piss bag
from bed to chair to door
complaining. She is unwilling
to rejoice as we do, finding her
here even as she fights
for pills for food for heat
caresses with eyes the faces
gathered around her bed
then turns away toward the wall
coughing. What means all this?

Nothing, says the red bird on the branch
darning winter out of the nest. Damn nothing.

A Friend

So little, her breath. When it stops
she falls. Her body all hinges. Bends
forward at the waist, sinks. Knees fold
out. The whole enterprise collapses.
Then rush to the pneumatic doors, Emergency,
the medical scurry. Needles, masks huffing,
and some kind of rescue without grace
or discernable plan. Not that they're paid
to care. No. Their real adrenalin is worry.

And you whom I love? Where are you? Where are you going?

Her account in the car. She feels as if she'll vomit and shit
at once. All the heat in her body rushes to her middle,
a wave of intense heat, and her fingers feel as if everything
essential is relinquishing them. She must be a writer leaving
her account of death behind. I'm listening and driving
at once, and we're both so calm. Two lively women,
in control. The young respiratory therapist has asthma.
She tells me I should have done better to bring her in
hours ago. We stay and watch but our listening is over.

Her Dream

Hyped on steroids for her lungs, she dreams:
the Commedia jester, my younger son,
transforms himself into the king;
alone, austere, his power evident
in his posture, conservative we might guess
from the cant of his shoulders under grape velvet.

He has chosen his counselors, these she spells out
as two, his nieces, tiny now but in the dream well grown.
They're warmly treated and received with love,
their parents in attendance, charming and respectful
to their king, their brother long denied, and to us both, old women.

She and I, she whispers, are there at court,
coifed blonde and brunette, laughs, too old to serve.
But we're draped in silks, sheer linens, fine wool
in winter in the shape of, she doesn't know the word
exactly, but tunic will do.

And we have, her voice lifts here, our choice
of dwellings: under a desert sun on stucco walls,
exquisite warmth on skull and hair. A benison.
Three good rooms for each. Everything we can use
we have at hand. We look just fine.

Our skin is older than it is now.
In our waking land, we're both in nightgowns talking on the phone,
she's seventy something and I'm some behind. But in her dream
our hawk's beaks are well defined. We have our choice
of jewels but no earrings grown too heavy for our lobes.

She talks for an hour then goes still.
As death turns the knob, she flings this fluency before him.

Objects When the Body Fails

1. *Eggs.*
Hard boiled, cooled, dunked into teacups
Of cellophane colors dissolved in vinegar.
Six for each child. In the center of the table
A pile of markers—many colored, stuffed in a jug.
Stickers, and scissors with red and orange handles,
The wire egg rack in the center lets the colored ones drip.
Each kid has deep grids on their knees.
Four kneel over a table covered in oilcloth.
Red, yellow, blue sails luff over the edges.
An adult in the back bedroom reads a book about soul.
In his thuddy chest a daughter rises like a rainbow egg
Lifted from her cup of vinegar bath.

2. *Pots with copper bottoms.*
One set for every house and one we suppose
For the nuns in their convent on the corner.
Pinky bottoms from lemon and salt
Or the chemical cleaner that fizzed dark
On the counter until washed off.
Peas steam in the pint with soda dissolved in water.
Better raw but not so digestible, served with butter.
Selma Levis used marge in the bag
We squished until the yellow blister popped
Under the thumb like bubblewrap, which came later.

3. *That one object made of rubber.*
Glue color, the shape of a capital O
Squished into an oval if you pushed just right.
Lived in a white plastic lid clipped over
The bottom then clicked closed. All powdery.
Discovered in the bedside table drawer.
Someone's mom said it had nothing to do with us.

4. "Particles," says Susan
When I ask what she's afraid of.
A fluidy rattle is her body's constant ground.
This time she's brief on the phone,
But I hear the workmen in the background
Grinding off plaster behind plastic sheets.
They use anchors to keep the plastic down:
A bottle of bleach, something called "All Solvent,"
And six bricks wrapped in beige linen napkins
Around the perimeter of her dining room.

5. Water.
When given a choice
Of water over air
We always picked water.
Maybe amnion was our model
Though we couldn't say why
Not even now, for the life of us.
I tried solving that riddle.
It's later, and we prefer air
Where we try to flourish
Like orchids on bark,
Our invisible support wires swaying
On currents from the wall vents.
Probably she'd like a river of air.
I wish I could give it to her.

6. Bed.
We all travel from.
Where are we going?
Her bedclothes are torchy brights, flowers
Under cashmere throws all teal and chili.
Her gowns are feathers.
She sleeps well and her dreams . . .
If I'm lucky, she tells me.

I report they're mostly the color
Of paprika on egg salad her mother fixed.

7. Roadside Attractions.
Good to soften the pain.
And movies, and soft foods
That sweeten as they go down.
Lotions, peppermint, visits
From friends, injections
Steroids or anaesthetics.
Books on tape or disk. Some paper.
A library card someone else uses.
A hang tag with a blue chair
In the car, for transportation.

Beloved, 24

Get in   with a packed suitcase to ride
the prairie rain-pocked   sleet marks the wide meadows
where is his body?   traveling   under shine it comes
in a nest of pleated linen   we return
in the wrong direction   then turn
to the sleety roads   toward your body
we breathe to hold away
what holds you fast   has come for you
        watch over you this cold evening as we go

we refuse to take up your absent wonder
we stand by your body as time takes you over
we are ice in the mud under your fingers
we refuse your breath   we will never leave you

Funeral, then Flu

Not the gym   Not the notebook   Not the streets   Not the
       block   Not the verge
Not the skyline   Not the midnight lights.

Service, service, service   blood on the knuckles   slice, grate, cut open,
       pour   dish
and spoon up and into, over

Nurses   friends   saints who eat drink   nothing. The neighbor
    dying young of cancer
to whose porch he brought   Thanksgiving dinner last year   the
       slices of ham   sweet potato   cranberries   nuts in a zippered
       bag   hard shelled sweets   pecan pie.
To the partner of the one
dying young of cancer
who does not eat.

Fever in the night   coughs   shivers   spewing   misery   and once
       you loved them all.
In the coffin
the body silver
as the boards. Silence

no rise nor fall
of the chest
the worker's hands
nails with their dark halos
yesterday he worked for a living.
Now purest absence.
Weeping and the rending of cloth.

We who can do no other
serve the living who can do no other

Fluids   electrolytes   sugars   salts.
Stir and mop up.   Collect wash
measure dry fold turn
and the best of us do it cold, cold.

Into the nests of bedclothes at night,
water bottles tissues books tapes creams
we rise at night in the next room
when the beloved cries out tosses
the memory
of the journey just over
the beloved youngster
dead in his coffin   silver
as his broken chest
father and lover
The same ears
of the one who spews
and suffers his fever
rising day after day
in flesh radiant enough you'd think
he could raise the dead in his arms one might think so,
measuring fever against the cold
the dead other who must begin
to generate heat through his icy stasis
creatures working
even as the other begins
to mend under the indifferent
care of the one who used to
love them both   who cares for
the quick and the dead
and can do no other
having made them
exactly with the body's instruction
who can do no other

but bend to the will
of the indifferent maker
who is said was said always
always to love them all.

Suite

1. Because rain fell all night
this morning the bird bath
in its ring of fragrant hostas
is filled to the brim. The rim barely
holds in the shining ring of water.
Part sun part shade is where
a half-dead apple tree leans;
light touches but barely
the tips of the branches
just at the edge of the garden.
Beyond the dapple
in full sun the old sandbox sits.
The upright swing next door
is just beginning to sound like calling
and the screen door closes and opens.

Suddenly after three aloof summers
the feral cat comes to sit on my lap
each morning at six, on white linen
where the bathrobe tie falls to my knees.
She brings her long claws and her sharp teeth
and the technology of her intermittent rumble.
Today she settles then turns to the window
where the wisteria drops its purple earrings
and they fall but not yet to the grass.

2. Look at this amaryllis! Three weeks ago
in the rush of holiday change
I whacked it good with a chair
took down the stem
opened a three-inch tear

and mostly severed the bud.
Should I throw it out? Cut the broken stem
to force in water? But I'm too busy
to do more than replace dirt in the plastic pot
then shove it into sun. I went to the kitchen, put up stew.

Aaron was surprised the morning of his leaving.
"Mom, plants heal," he told me. I'd forgotten.
So here it is, ready to bloom:
Three fat buds each three inches long
and the tears healed. Straight stem.
Not exactly beautiful, not callas from the florist
but maybe one of those signs and wonders
we can use? I don't know exactly but figure you will.

3. Early morning in June
White linen robe
gift ten years ago
in the pocket
white linen square
bordered with lace
my grandmother made
half a century ago
transferred from her drawer
to my suitcase after death.
I reach in order
to blot my face.

The flax swaying in the fields,
The loom at its work,
The plant fiber transforming,
Those at work breathing,
Touching thread, the winding
Sheet and the binder

The moment beyond this breath

4. I've put up chili, or what looks like chili,
added eggplant diced and fresh rosemary
from the patio flat. The tomatoes mask
additions so we'll never know that coffee
makes the vegetables float. Already August.
Squirrels scurry acorns on the bricks into pots
of dying geraniums and whatever hurls itself
down makes the usual noise. Loud the cat
about her silvery mouse on the indoor tiles. Look
out the window at that sunshine. Still summer.
Who can know what's ending
over land where the uncut hair of graves
waits to be measured, plowed, then opened?

    5. Her Ghazal
The season turns at last.
You ask me a question, why last?

The gingko accepts snow's burden.
No matter, limbs bow at last,

Or trees crack. Yesterday you made a visit.
After surgery, morphine, stitches out at last.

Silence is news. Meat in the sink, signs of sustenance.
Signs that ask, Does life transfer at the last?

Bodies in bed take such a small space.
Two sticks, we will be given away at last.

Or go fast alone. Some miracle. The sky is dark.
Now morning. What's left? You alive, at last.

Again

Friendship, like the immortality of the soul, is too good to be believed.
—RALPH WALDO EMERSON, "On Love and Friendship"

Do you suppose you could be wheeled to the garden?
Would you like to listen to Bach's cello concertos?
Do you think chilled grapes would make you happy?
Does your mother's voice call you to childhood naps?
Does sleep all afternoon invite your cotton counterpane?
Will voices reading to you compromise your journey?

Remember warmth stored in sand when you're lying by
    the ocean?
Imagine your first dress from childhood's celebrations!
Dust the toes of your first pair of patent leather slippers.
Look into the reflection in the birdbath on the porch railing.
Growl with the dog, who wants to taste your dinner.
Speak up when silence overtakes you. Enter silence like a lover.

We're angry when they leave. They're angry when you do.
Know that the ending of bereavement must always be reunion.

Can afternoon light find your pillow?
Who strokes your hair when your face is damp?

Palms rinsed with tepid water can sometimes return the favor.

Her Dying

You will die soon. We all die.
We all go out from our houses.
My house, for example, is Willow Grove.
Your house—you still have one—is Garland Place.
The roofs are yellow, a tile called Cyon Picaresque.
Hang on or

You'll slip or
You're falling
Into the run off.
The white rabbit
Your heart
Thuds blue, tart prickles, burnt
Towers in the far garden. Prairie overtakes your bed.

Now you're coming alive,
Scioto pears in your palms,
Your nightgown, your slippers, your hair-ribbon
Resolving into wet ash.
We've tried to
Reach you, stitch pain
Into bread for you.
Once we walked together in the garden
Our sons ahead and behind us . . .
Something soothes so smartly since sunup . . .
Look at that orchid
On your tongue it tastes like heaven
You reach for   pricked pull away.

You're becoming the polished boards of grief
collapsing into the house they
Now look! A soaring over the rooftops with legs
Flapping, warping air as it goes,
A zigzaggedy culvert of bird-Vs.
You go west from Garland, they go south.
We on Bread Street watch
You leave, hear your breathy messages lapse
Into mountains of sibilants hush hush.
Do not go without us
We call into your growing silence,
but you go, cease,
ceding yourself with your breath to us.

The Changes

Everything we promised you was so
is not. Wounds filled with your blood
leak out their bandages so your gown
is rosy wet. Your frail spouse
who begged for news, our promise
that he would not have to watch
or lift the gauze, was told good news.
We lied. Each day he tears the tape,
repacks what used to be your breast.

What we said to you was not is so:
pain's presence where you have no flesh,
numb where what is left is still intact.
No one who breathes can be your friend
least one, who lives and knows
and will not tell.

Where yesterday they bent to kiss
your breast today is gone, missed
every minute dissolved in sound
throat alters; breath is drowned
then rescued, lost again. We make of this
truth what we will. I cry now because I can.

A Body of Water

after Donald Hall, for KN

Lake air   dusk
warm outside   cool in the house.
On the rock   table   residue
of redwood, hemlock, spruce.
High over the water   window
teak table   rubbed linseed   seventy years.
Everything round   lake   table
mats   water carafe   the pot
for sugar, crystal shot glass for salt,
silver spoons   their bowls tucked
into sweet and brine. Eyes red with both.

A slow wind   here the trumpet vine fallen
with its struts, there an azalia twelve feet around.
Two tin olive cans strung on cable
moving from the center of the window,
bisected wood, the eaves with their eight struts.
In twenty years the trees have risen.

Wind breathes
needles soften on their branches.
The house holds, houses do, the contour of ground,
clay holds the new fence at garden's edge where it was.
The light ripens late tomatoes   rhubarb
by the stable doors, Pickpocket gone, new wood.

Now the lake stirs, wind, diagonal ripples
laze and hit the old dock. Open gate
white against the color of wood chips
pine needles   the gazebo filled to the tenth log,
oh children children   and Squash the dog, Buttons the cat.

Not crystal the vase made by a child,
not daisy   an open geranium in blue pottery
cream drips the color of petals
the bud of the geranium   unopened green
center rose red   years ago daisy shading toward yellow
sky gray   then late sun on the dock, oh come out
come out.

Someone has died. She was a woman
who'd forgotten her name. The names of her children.
Her companion. Her life. Eggplant, rosemary, wind, blue.
But a restless roaming. Vernon, Dale, Ron, Merle.

Elegy for Two Poets

S and R

The pet calls
but no, the silver bowl is full
and the woolen throw at the foot
of the bed is pulled askew.
On the roof
sliding ice into slow melt
makes water accumulate somewhere
beyond gutters' overflow.
At the junction
of star and sky a flash like electricity
arcs into fuse before fire rages.
Pilot, we call as we rush higher.

There is a great river called
what. Where will you cross
when you have put down your pots and pens,
whose maps to guide your powdered inks?

We cannot endure it, these deaths like paper
put to the flood, the breath all gone so decay sets in
at the juncture of breastbone and rib, the emptying
cavities where color freshens. Your words un-
braid like hair put to the match, fused. Underneath, not even a body
of water to tear into banks, no bridge to construct from spent
        matches.

And your children are dead, the boys who grew
in the purses of your bodies, now ash as the grate grows hot.
Not time enough to push and spin at once, not words and flesh
at once, not courage and porridge, not portage against the flood,

no help to pack or arrange for details, the sharpened knife,
  the static truck.

We who spit into the ink pot for you, we dip our braids
to make your route with the powders of your leaving,
trace the river bank, then get up to carry brick to keep
back the melt of ice from foundations, we breathe
as best we can from our drying lungs, to keep you
just a while longer, a month? May we have you
for a day, an hour, the minutes we use up in words
to remember the flash of your freshening minds
at play in the language, how warm your shoulders
holding us, saying hello, saying thank you, goodbye?

V
THE ESPECIAL SHAPE

2 A.M. Migraine

Is this the blue hour, no.
But the cat in her six fur bodies
leads a way out of bed to the kitchen.
Absinthe of the middle years, the queen's kingdom.

The gold overhead light steadies under the switch.
I am not buried in oiled pearwood yet.
Night's veils will part.
A book's pages fly to my prints.

At the corners of my eyes
bright flashes signal the night jaguar pacing off her black café.

Moving Pictures

"The Maquettes of Robert Arneson"

With a wooden paddle
the size of a bat
he hits the clay head hard.
Feathery eyebrows
then his unglazed eye.
Who is this old man,
his dare, his frizz of hair,
his doctor's coat?

"Make comment on human fallacies without concession,
whistling the while," he says to the camera.

He's a little overweight
slightly paranoid
and arrogant, he says.
Why play it safe?
"Clay can't hurt you,
it's pretty informal."

Who was it developed the glaze
in his mainstream?
Maybe bladder cancer
made his face fall into
tile at pool's bottom
and just stay wet? His own neck's
jerked off every caryatid
Splat! on the hard piazza floor
and the head still laughing.

No decay possible
when everything's
fired. Such a huge kiln
to open on your own face!

Dark Haired, Dark Eyed, Fierce

When the photographer came
she asked him how to appear
in charge, the commander poised,
a female authority, and he said,
"Cross your arms over your chest
and raise your chin." She did
on every website hit for months
through four strong seasons and the fall.
Now in this ad she's wearing red,
arms and legs akimbo, her four-inch
left shoe's heel pushed into her kneecap,
the neck's fur scarf dripping past her lap
to crotch. The legs are open.
Her nails are bare, her eyes veiled
only by cropped hair in Theda Bara fringe,
in shadow, ringed with kohl.

                    What are we advancing here,
all four limbs bent in puppet disarray?
A female pliancy? The yoga's payoff?
Are we still fierce, in dyed red seal
that's edged with kid, Gianfranco Ferre,
suspended in your transparent vinyl egg?
My undershirt and briefs are net. The fur
beneath the fur is brown.

Professional Travel

Tomorrow we must pack.
Competition is the reason for this meeting. We're scared
silly to be flinging
linen and denim into a suitcase,
pushing the hard lid closed.

By evening all open minds will close.
Old friends in the lobby pack
each other's ears with greetings. Competition
is the order of the day, whose suitcase
is more costly, whose new contract scares
us silly with envy until we're flinging

praise around, or starting a fling
with the hot new painter, closing
out others whose silence, artist's block, is scary
or maybe contagious? Look! There's Horace Pack
alive at sixty, his leather suitcase
and jacket matching. This year he's no competition

for the Writer's Prize. But life's no competition
for him after near-death. For him a fling
is a metaphor for breathing. He's pushing a suitcase
on wheels, heavy with books, carefully closed
on his wife's artful packing.
Being here is no scare

for him, really, no scare
for us, either. Competition
rides our blood, arteries packing
danger into an adrenaline fling.
Earlier episodes cauterized are closed
in a title, "Ashes in a Suitcase,"

red tag attached to a black suit on the cover, in the suitcase.
Name and address flaunt our location, the world. We're not scared,
but filled with essential knowledge, closed
off from the company. Winning the near-death competition
one year is no guarantee—we know it—only a fling
with a new lover. We're not ready to go. But the suitcase is packed

or unpacked, whatever. Fear's unavailable for reuse in the competition.
Scared or not, we're here, maybe that's the point. Fling
that suitcase from the platform! Know that the damned lid is closed.

Alice

What we call history is nothing more than a continuum—in
reverse gear—of the present. —ALICE STEINBACH

I.

Continual occupation and change
weaken one's sense of one's feelings
so looking forward to something
—a dinner at Orchids's for example—
can distract from impatience, the desire
to see you again, which may lead to
—which impression must I want to convey?—
boredom or disappointment since the future
might be considered a department store
of choices, luxury goods I want to own
and use up. A black Armani suit
for example, perfect for the lecture circuit
beginning in October, or the cocktail hour
I enter without you, or the art opening
where we go together in our jeans.
Surely I feel something, don't I,
a kind of ennui, impatience
at forgetting the location of the suitcase?

2.

My feeling this afternoon—the blue hour, no?
is like yours, or Billie Holiday's as her eyes
roll up into that note we hear from the balcony
above the thump and below the machinery's
back-up beep. We feel something, surely,
on vacation from our continual preoccupation
with change. Don't we? The extra rich ice cream
melting? Peppermint panties? Ads for pain killers
plugging into our anxiety exactly as arteries slam shut?

3.

You asked. Here are my impressions. Rushing forward
backward gets us nowhere. We're all alone
with these big possibilities. Talk is expensive
but we can pay the bill. Can't we? Our waiter is drugged.
This soup is delicious. Pale beets, imagine.
These earrings of gold seeds and calcedony are lovely.

4.

At four when I wake the door is still open
to the balcony. Police helicopter? No lights.
Fire? Someone is missing? A wind.
My heart is occupied to the tune
of the blades—thwup, thwup. A mystery.
Thanks, Nancy Drew, but I'm sick
of preoccupations, appointments to deconstruct
the story shuffling through the SONY PSYC.
I can, you know, so well trained
nothing narrative escapes analysis. Am I correct?
Am I cold? How much do you charge to cuddle?
No wonder we like the feral cat who stays
only long enough to drool before fear takes over.

5.

You're here but you're furniture,
a leather sofa that springs open into a bed.
You could be anyone so long as you hold up the nightclothes.
We've had a chat over excellent veal
pounded sliver thin. Yes, we're both against war,
big business, wind power, and material goods from China
if they're shoddy and poor design. We agree
it's best to stay thin. Ghandi said eating meat
incites lust, didn't he? You've got mud on your boots.
In my house you'd have to go around or take them off.
Yes, I see they're a fine design, leather gloves

for feet, durable and not synthetic.
I'm tired. Where did you say you're going?
Shall we share a cab?

6.

Her "storytelling voice is just as strong as her drawing grammar." —ALICE

Subtract one and you've got, what?
Half a talent? Half a couple,
one of whom shoots the dogs?
I promise to stay put if you do
but how? Something about big
machinery, a helicopter doing our work
on a tiny laptop connected to wind, your weather blog?
Talk to me! Oh, I forgot our subject, three restaurants:
"a table is an altar," says the Talmud. Twice a week we worship.
I'm sad to be throwing out my storytelling voice
over pizza and beer, hoping you'll deploy
your drawing grammar in a way I recognize.

7.
Once a time lapse is enough,
isn't it? My favorite suitcase is red,
a portmanteau into which stuff goes,
the necessities for a good visit.
Seven days' purge through the portals of the ear
means a stream rushing on down the mountain
below this balcony. Still sitting here
this morning, thank God for the ascent
made by the cable car fifteen times already.
What are you doing? Thinking about me?
Alice goes to her room.
Travel without the beloved is travel in letters
on the page. Is that it? Never, never, never,
never, never said Lear over the body of his daughter.

8.

Did you have a good trip? she asks
as she hands out soap, hard currency for gifts
to distribute generously. Here the mountain air is chilly.
Are you surprised? I sit reading on the balcony
overlooking three mountains merged, like cleavage.
Late in the day we might drink champagne. It's fall,
another end or a beginning. We've brought clothes
we've never worn, pack up piece by piece through hours.
Alice is traveling in Provence, alone or with a learned guide.
Soon we'll decide now is exactly the right time to go home.

VI
ALL ODD AND SPLENDID

Terza Rima

Where to begin this morning, Sunday eve?
With death? He did, she did, I will
or no. Be blunt. The kitchen knife.

The rope in the garage. The window sill's
shards of broken glass. The hot rail
in the middle of the subway. Pills.

Against all I wedge a plastic pail
filled up with sea, my cousins tugging
at the handle, hot sand absorbing water.

Then the sunrise. Dependable plug
for despair, for fear, for other indignities
that keep us shivering under covers.

Like you? Like him? Like one
who does the shopping, buys the flowers
in their simple pots, lifts the roast into the pan?

God! We rise, put on the coffee pot, shower
and dry this body, lift up the window to smell snow.
Where can we find spice in this, or power?

On coasts of air, in shoals of coral, with winds that blow
the fog away so landing lights make out the runways
as we land tomorrow? Dear Lady to all this saying no

I beg indulgence, forgiveness, insurance, and the blight
that leaves no scar on those we love, but only on my shoulders
rounding as they take on weight, the trip I'll make

By air, this time. The lift-off shocking,
the plane turning its back on sun, traveling
west in early morning, racing somewhere.

Sunrise, bird breath visible in cold, the children's chant,
earth turning, the Pleiades, the goddesses and their dogs,
the mind at work, the body's song, the water in the pail,
    the warming sand.

Now

It's Fourth of July
again where shall we go
up the high crest of the hill
to watch or onto the driveway
where kids crouch to light
God knows what special effects
in the dark mosquito hum?

This year the velvet quiet
drops like too much cover
too hot when you want
to stretch out but can't.
Something alive nuzzles
your side keeping company
with the old body until you love
too warm. The silence stays put.
If you lie still and breathe
soon the small chill of midnight
will find your pillow.

Tenor Part

The thistle in the border
behind the tree peony
whistles a riff on the subject
of succor: expect none from me,
he says as light folds down
over the flap of the patio.
I who sit waiting
for fear to stop
attend to the spikes
and the bud brush
not yet ready.

Learn, croons the garden
from its fringe of weeds, Lamia
stretched over the brick walks,
the Periwinkle vine mat
strangling Lilies-of- the-valley.
Late in the afternoon, as it is,
the wind makes cream
from the seeding Dandelions
and in Italian pots the expensive
Geraniums push forward their lavenders
and neons to reach for the sun's last rays.

Splendid

Now she's sick, cut.
He almost died but didn't.

Is my baby ugly? he whispers.
I answer here. No.

His arms are short. Her neck wobbles.
What's the matter? Everything.

For twelve days and nights the wisteria
grows tricolored lamps on twisted branches
that cast no light to read by.
Each year we sit on a bench reading.
We sit still.

If he lies on the floor and hums
If she builds towers and bridges with her fingers
If grey light bleeds lavender onto the pages
What can be said to be missing? What else can matter?

Love This

early morning light, the chant of the cat,
coffee hot with milk, chenille royal purple
heat against cold, the dying dead,
children safe & far away, the children's children

coffee hot with milk, chenille a royal purple
evergreen sprigs in the bittersweet wreath
children safe but far away, the children's children
safe in their beds where I can't see

coffee black, chenille rags of royal purple
children safe but far away, the children's children
evergreen sprig in the bittersweet wreath
seasons change but I'm still alive

children safe but far away, the children's children
the clock ticks out, clicks time over
seasons change and I still alive
have bags to pack, worlds to write.

The clock rolls over but still some time
heat against cold, the dying dead
bags to pack, words to write
early morning light, the chant of the cat.

Thank You Very Much

Never, never, never, never, never—KING LEAR

indeed for the mush giant Hosta become with frost,
for mighty fine women up from their beds to put on coffee,
for chores reduced by cold, for cold nights lengthened at the hem.

Thank you very much for undertaking this audition,
for entertainment unraveling five rows back and center,
for free tickets' admission to the big ones, birth and passion,
for novels uncut; for heads unencumbered, as yet ungarlanded,

for the unanswered phone, the instruments in the band not warming up.

Thank you too for the filled freezer,
the fur parka, the dead animals on the verge big ones this season,
for sweaters at discount, stores filled with designer clothing,
for thousand-dollar vacuum cleaners, for used cars with not much
        mileage,
for unnecessary telephone poles in subdivisions,
for cell phones that vibrate, for leather upholstery,
for toothbrushes and green toothpaste from Maine, for undeclared wars,
for braces on limbs and teeth, for surgery, for sutures,
for stents and staples, for health insurance,
for generation, for shoelaces, for tap dancing
for love for love for love for love, for love.

CREDITS AND ACKNOWLEDGMENTS

Thanks to the editors of these and other journals and anthologies in which my poems were published, sometimes in earlier versions:

"Pets," *Contemporary Poetry by Nebraskans*, ed. Mary K. Stillwell, Denise Banker, and Greg Kosmicki, Backwaters Press, 2008
"Arousal" and "Beloved, 24," *Blue Mesa Review*
"Complaint," *The Cincinnati Review*
"Spring Snowstorm" and "Tenor Part," *Crazed by the Sun: Poems of Ecstasy*
"Splendid," *Margie*
"Spring Snowstorm" and "Paper Strip," *Mid-American Review*
"Elegy for Two Poets," *New Millennium Writings: 2006–07*
"September 11" and "Diaspora," *Nightsun 25*, ed. Alicia Ostriker
"Vocation," "He Graduates from Clown School," and "Son," *Paterson Literary Review 36*
"All Odd and Splendid," "Dante's Words," "Funeral, then Flu," Terza Rima," *Paterson Literary Review 35*
"Once," *Paterson Literary Review 31*
"Thank You Very Much," "Son," "Alice" (published as "Negotiations"), "Vocation" (published as "Knowing"), *PoetryMagazine.com*
"Sunday Morning, without Couplet," *Pleiades*
"Water Ceremonies," "Wilt," "He/She: The Bike," "Son," *SALT Magazine*
"A Body of Water," *SALT Magazine*; reprinted in *The Sorrow Psalms*, ed. Lynn Strongin, University of Iowa Press, 2008
"Her Dream" and "Coma," *The Women's Review of Books*, 2008

Many voices in these poems: Aaron Raz Link told me "Tyr." He is everywhere here. Anna and Eva Shoenhammer Link speak in their own voices or through their papa, John Link. "An Evening" is for John Link. All transcriptions and additions are mine, faults and infelicities too.

To brilliant companions and collaborators, all thanks. Grace Bauer, Steve Behrendt, Burke and Laura Rhodes Casari, Vera Spohr Cohen, Pat Emile, Lisa Linsalata, Wanda Freeman, John Kinsella, Eric Levy, Anna Link, Eva Link, Chad Nordyke, Carole Simmons Oles, Susan Atefat Peckham, JoAn Rittenhouse, Susan Rosowski, Maria Schoenhammer, Suzanna Tamminen, and Reetika Vasarini are in these pages. Jonis Agee and Sharon Oard Warner provide their warm support to many writers, including me. Janet Burroway and Floyd Skloot made this book possible. Dale, John, and Aaron are the matrix. This book is for them and for all our family and friends.

HILDA RAZ is the author of many books of poetry including two published with Wesleyan University Press, *Divine Honors* (1997), and *Trans* (2001). She is Professor of English and women's and gender studies at the University of Nebraska–Lincoln where she is the Luschei Editor for *Prairie Schooner*. With her son Aaron Raz she has written a memoir, *What Becomes You,* on the subject of his sex change (Univerity of Nebraska Press, 2008). The book was a finalist for the Lambda Book Award and was published in the American Lives Series edited by Tobias Wolff for the University of Nebraska Press.